BROKEN
like everybody else

A Memoir of Trauma
and Redemption

Jose Del Cueto

HP

Hawkeye Publishers

Broken Like Everybody Else:
A Memoir of Trauma and Redemption

Special thanks to Travis Gale for fonts contributed to cover design.

For more information, please address Hawkeye Publishers
P.O. Box 3098, Camarillo, CA 93011.

Library of Congress Control Number: 2017951807

Paperback: 978-1-946005-14-4
Hardcover: 978-1-946005-15-1
Ebook: 978-1-946005-17-5

HawkeyePublishers.com

Big thanks to
Andrea Billups

Miss Andrea is a journalism teacher and a
great author with well-deserved national acclaim.
She is an exceptional human being who
guided me and helped with this book.

I hope our friendship lasts a lifetime.

Thank you, Miss Andrea!

With my dad, 1958

Broken Contents

With my wife Cindy, 1992

Introduction

This is my story of dealing with trauma-induced learning disabilities, and why I've generally struggled so much throughout my life.

All challenges aside, however, I've still somehow managed to stay married to the same brilliant woman for more than thirty-five years. With her blessings, I left my cushy life to go back to college for the first time in decades, and that's when I discovered something huge about myself: that I was broken. Even though I've gained professional success and raised three great kids over the years, I was working with shattered and emotionally-damaged pieces for a very long time.

Many people sense that something is wrong with them, and they need answers to help them lead better lives. My intention in writing this book is to encourage and help those people, not to disparage anyone.

These pages recount events to the best of my recollection, but some names and places have been changed to protect innocent bystanders.

Here's to a better life!

—Joe Del Cueto

College football game, 2016

Chapter 1

59 and Back in College

It's August in Gainesville, Florida, and there's a new sense of purpose in the air. The fall semester at the University of Florida has begun, and football season is about to kick off. It's a thick and scorching summer, seemingly a thousand degrees in the shade.

I'm dizzily trekking across campus while hundreds of kids are running around me, moving at warp speeds on foot, bikes, skateboards, or scooters. They effortlessly swarm through this giant maze of a campus with confidence, knowing exactly what to do and where to go. They are happy.

But I am not.

My heart is pounding. I am terrified. I'm trying to find my way to a classroom with no idea if I'm going to get there in time. I don't remember it being this difficult nearly 40 years ago when I was last a student.

"Why in the world have I done this to myself?" I mutter as sweat rolls beneath my collared golf shirt.

I am neither a gym rat, a frat guy, nor some kid who just got his high school diploma nine months ago, so I refuse to wear shorts despite the heat. My greatest fear isn't how I look or smell -which must be awful- but the very good chance that I will pass out.

My anxiety rages. I am out of my element, outside my comfort zone, and worlds away from anything that feels safe.

When I was here forty years ago, I was an uninterested student from Miami, culturally adrift, impatient, and not really learning a damned thing.

"Please, God. Don't let me faint."

I'm naive as hell, carrying a fifty-pound backpack with every single textbook and notebook that I own. Nobody told me that you don't need to bring your textbooks with you. I'm completely disoriented, and after asking a few kids for directions, I learn that my next class is clear across campus; a thirty-minute hike in the heat.

I feel the blood throbbing in my temples. "I am going to have a heart attack right here in the middle of all of this. Wouldn't that be something?!"

"Slow down. Slow down. Breathe."

I tell myself this is the same recurring nightmare that I've had for decades. I MUST be dreaming all of this. I will wake up, and when I do, I'll be Joe again, a successful business owner, fifty-nine years old, with no need to go back to school. I live in beautiful Miami and the Florida Keys, and this is just a nightmare...

...except it isn't. The sweat drips onto my hand and I wipe it on my pants. My chest tightens, and I shift my backpack like a soldier hiking through the desert.

This situation is real, and so is my brewing panic attack. I am here! I put myself here, and it is not imaginary.

I wonder if anyone will notice if I drop to the ground.

Fight it. Keep walking. Just make it to class.

I trudge along, lost in my head, and breathing heavily. Avoiding eye contact with everyone around me, I finally make it to class somehow, with a minute to spare.

The air-conditioned lecture hall revives me. I sink into a seat in the back of the room, and jam my giant backpack behind the row of auditorium chairs in front of me. I imagine nearly everyone is staring at me, and

I know what they're thinking: "What is DAD doing in my class, dude?"

I look around and somehow manage a half-smile as I wipe my brow and tidy up to the best of my ability.

I want to focus. I want to belong. Failing is not an option. I will graduate. I am Joe; I'm smart and competent and a winner.

So...why did I do this to myself?

Gainesville, Florida, 2016

Chapter 2

Then to Now

Coral Gables is one of the nicest neighborhoods in Miami. Up until a month ago, I lived there in a gorgeous house.

My neighbors were famous telenovela stars, musicians, and millionaires. There was a pool, a hot car, nice landscaping, and palm trees.

That was the 'normal' I had worked for, and I loved the life that my wife and I have made for ourselves.

If weekdays weren't nice enough in our comfortable abode, I also kept a boat and a condo on the water in the Florida Keys, and could go there on the weekends to relax.

It was perfect.

And yet...there was something missing; some unfinished business that nagged at me like a quiet voice in the back of my mind.

In the seventies I had moved far away from my friends and culture in Miami, and enrolled as an advertising student at the University of Florida (UF). It was a strange transition for a boy from Puerto Rico. I missed the food, the music, and the brown people with names like Hernandez.

My professor pulled me aside one day and told me: "Joe, you're not cut out for an advertising career. You need to think about doing something else." I was hurt, but I knew he was probably right; I was not doing well in school.

So I dropped out.

I had ultimately let myself down by quitting something that I knew I could finish; I'd let someone else define my future. And that wasn't like me; I have always defined my own life.

Years later, through dedication and sheer will, I eventually became a millionaire, brokering advertising deals in Europe, South America, and New York. As it turned out, I was actually really good at advertising after all, but I was still a college dropout.

My drive comes from a unique background: I was born in Havana, Cuba, on August 15, 1957. My father, José Alberto Del Cueto, was an MIT-educated engineer from a prominent Cuban family that included famous political figures, business leaders, and intellectuals. He was an Olympian who had represented Cuba in skeet shooting.

In contrast, my mother Aida was the daughter of a middle-class movie theater owner and a stay-at-home mom. My parents' marriage was of "un-evens" and perhaps destined to fail.

I was not only their third and youngest child, but perhaps most relevant to my upbringing, their only boy. There was tension in my parents' marriage even prior to my birth. My mother had given birth to two daughters before me who were five and ten years older than I. And like many men of his era, my dad was disappointed not to have a male heir.

In fact, when my second sister was born, my father refused to go to the hospital to see his newborn daughter. But when I was born, he was elated. He thought of me as the special child; the long-awaited baby boy.

My mother, on the other hand, was resentful and had mixed feelings about me, at best. She likely felt forced to continue having children until one of them was a boy. As I look back on her dilemma and pressure, I truly feel for her.

By the time I was two years old, I had become my family's little prince, the anointed one, the carrier of the Del Cueto name. The first two years of my life in Cuba were magical. My father, his family, and all of his friends were overjoyed to finally dote on a son.

I was, without a doubt, spoiled rotten, and got every toy I ever wanted. My father often showed up with a new gift for me and nothing for my sisters, which created a real divide in our home. I didn't realize it at the time, of course, but now, looking back I realize this wasn't fair; my father was wrong for doing that.

Our lives were still charmed. Each of us -my sisters and I- had a personal nanny. But since the nanny took care of my every need, I didn't notice the growing distance between my mother and me. I have no recollection of my mother ever carrying me, other than holding me in the occasional family portrait. There was an unmistakable disconnect between us that would persist throughout my life.

Even as a child I wondered if my mother loved me. I knew exactly how my father felt and what I meant to him, but I couldn't make sense of my mother's behavior.

In later years I would learn that my parents had a terrible marriage, and that they barely liked each other, let alone loved one another.

Three years after my birth, the Castro Revolution in Cuba was in full swing. My mother decided to leave Cuba and move us to Chicago, where some of her family had resettled. Her brother, sister, and parents had been living in the suburbs of Chicago for a few years. They had somehow foreseen the coming revolution and escaped Cuba while they could.

I arrived in Chicago barely three years old, to what I would generously call a "hostile environment." My mother used me as a pawn of sorts to pressure my father to join us in Illinois.

All the people who loved me and considered me a prince were thousands of miles away. My mother's side never warmed up to me because I was a spitting image of my father, representing everything that had gone badly for their Aida.

My father frequently wrote me letters from Cuba, but even that caused problems because he never wrote any for my sisters. Being only three years old, I needed someone to read the letters to me, and my grandmother was the only one willing to do it. No one else wanted to support what they saw as my father's blatant show of favoritism.

It was a difficult adjustment to make; I'd gone from living a luxury Cuban life as a prince, to an immigrant in Illinois during the dead of winter, freezing my ass off, without a friend in sight.

Even though I was very young, I had to learn to defend myself because my cousins and sisters constantly bullied me, taunting me by asking, "Where's your daddy now?"

I was always a hyper child and I quickly became a rebellious one as well. After breaking my arm while horsing around one time, I used the cast as a weapon, swinging it to keep my cousins and sisters away.

When I look back, one thing stands out about that period in my childhood: my grandfather was the only man I recall taking the time to play with me, or even care for me. His actions were not very popular with his children or other grandchildren, yet he showed me real love. He went against the grain, nurturing me with attention and affection, and this wouldn't be the last time he did so.

Things started to look up when my father decided to join us in Chicago. To me that was a sign of possible good times ahead, but life in the Windy City was difficult for him. He was a stranger in a strange land, and treated with hostility by my mother's family.

Although my father wanted no part of this frozen tundra, he placed our needs before his own dreams in an attempt to put the family back together. He eventually decided to move us all somewhere warmer, to Mexico City, where he had found a job at the National Cigar Company.

My father also brought his sister, nieces, and widowed mother to Mexico. I was excited to be the "little prince" once again, surrounded by people who loved me. My father and grandmother, in particular, thought I could do no wrong.

I have very fond memories of our short stay in Mexico City. I went to Kindergarten during the day, and then headed to my grandmother's house, where she would spoil me with toys and candy.

Every weekend in Mexico felt like a new adventure. Given that my father was an avid sportsman, shooter, hunter, race car driver, and fisherman, spending time around him was every little boy's dream.

It was always just me and my father on those excursions; the girls would be left behind. I only remember a handful of family outings where all of us were together, and the divide in the family continued to grow.

My father, being a well-educated executive in Mexico, quickly made friends with the Mexican elite as well. Years later, one of Mexico's wealthiest businessmen, called my mother after my dad passed away, and offered to raise me if my mother wanted to send me back to Mexico. These were the strong friendships that my father created everywhere he went; he was amazing.

But my mother hated living in Mexico, so she threatened to leave with the children once again if my dad didn't make a move.

Fearing another split, my father had two choices: we could either move to Nigeria, where there was a growing tobacco industry, which would make it easy for him to find work, or we could go to Puerto Rico, where some of the college-educated Cuban exiles were building a community.

I don't know which one of my parents made the final decision, but Nigeria was ruled out.

Chapter 3

Tragedy in Puerto Rico

I certainly didn't know it when we first arrived in Puerto Rico in 1964, but my family would end up living there for fifty-plus years. All I knew at the time was that I was officially a "Cubarrican," even though I didn't feel like one at all.

It was a difficult adjustment, both culturally and emotionally, and my family struggled to make things work. I began first grade at the same Catholic school where my mother had taken a job as a typing teacher. My father had a hard time finding a job at first because tens of thousands of other college-educated Cubans arrived in Puerto Rico around the same time as us.

During this era, Cubans in Puerto Rico were seen as a threat to the existing Puerto Rican managerial class. They were highly educated, had lost everything, been exiled from their country, and they were extremely eager to get ahead. Many Cuban professionals like my dad inevitably displaced Puerto Ricans from their jobs. It was not a friendly environment.

As is frequently the case with immigrants, all the recently-arrived Cubans were living in the same neighborhoods, therefore attending the same schools and frequenting the same beaches.

A dear family friend with his wife and five children lived with us for over a year while they saved up to get their own place. Twelve of us were sharing a three-bedroom, two-bathroom apartment. It was a very noisy and busy household.

My father was determined to make things work, so he had two jobs at the same time. The first, his day job, was as a draftsman at a local engineering firm, a job for which he was wildly overqualified. And his second job was in the nearby mountains, growing experimental tobacco as he was trying to launch his own business. Both practical and entrepreneurial, he made a deep impression on me that I eventually carried into my own business life.

Dad and I used to play together in our front yard every day, throw darts, play catch, and shoot my BB gun. Sometimes his friends would join us, and it was pure heaven. On the weekends we would get into my dad's Volkswagen Beetle and drive to the other side of the island to visit my dad's cousin. It was a lot of fun!

On some weekends my father took me to the mountains, where together with his friends and their sons, we would all go duck hunting. It was a great father/son bonding activity, and I had plenty of kids to play with as well.

One particular Saturday, my dad and I left the house as usual, except this time I was taken to what looked like a military training camp. A bunch of Cuban men without their children were dressed in full camouflaged gear, armed with assault rifles. Years later, my mother told me that my father had been involved with the counterrevolution in Cuba, collaborating with the U.S. Government in various capacities. They were being trained by the CIA for what would become the Bay of Pigs Invasion.

Little had changed between my parents from our time in Mexico City. My father continued to exclude my mother and sisters, and I continued to enjoy these boys' weekends with him, completely unaware of the pain they were causing at home.

Nonetheless, my mother and sisters, cousins, grandparents, and aunts, all held the tight bond that I had with my dad against me. I became an easy target, re-directing their anger with my father towards me. I felt pulled back and forth, not really understanding how a kid could cause such ire.

My father didn't seem bothered by this inequality. He thought that watching a replica of himself grow up was the greatest possible gift. If I had to do it all again, I would still honor the privilege of receiving my father's love, of course, but I'd wish a different fate for my mother and sisters. As a child, I wasn't able to understand or change any of it. And as a parent later on, I subconsciously focused on my two daughters, and left my only boy to become strong on his own.

I realize how fortunate I was. All those moments with my father ultimately shaped me. I am who I am because of what he taught me back then. My dad will never know how grateful I truly am. He'll never know that those years of standing by his side allowed me to stand tall throughout my life. For all his faults, I am proud of being Pepe Del Cueto's son.

The last time I saw him alive was the morning of February 23, 1965. We had breakfast together before I went to school, and he headed off to work. From that day on, my life spiraled downhill for a long time.

I was only eight years old, but I remember that day as if it was last week. After school I went straight to my friend's house to play basketball, but when I saw a parade of familiar cars driving in the direction of my house, I quickly ran home through people's backyards. I found my mother crying hysterically on the porch with some friends and neighbors consoling her. I knew that something catastrophic had happened, and it didn't take me long to figure out that my father had died.

He had suffered a massive brain hemorrhage at age thirty-nine (presumably the result of lasting damage from a racing car accident years before). He was at his tobacco farm when he collapsed. An ambulance rushed him to two different hospitals that rejected him for being an uninsured immigrant, and he died in the ambulance on their way to a third.

As was customary back then, children were isolated from death, so my family did not take me to the funeral, nor did I get to see my dad in his casket. That experience robbed me of closure. I was expected to simply move on. Those unresolved emotions chased after me for years, presenting themselves in much uglier ways in an effort to work themselves out. It would be a very long time before I discover a healthy way to grieve, and a better way to live.

From the moment of my father's death, playing guitar became my saving grace. It would sustain me through the hurricane I was about to face.

Just days before my dad passed away, he signed a life insurance policy that helped my mother make ends meet for years to come.

Despite this small fortune, my mother was now a thirty-nine-year-old widow living in a foreign country with three kids. She refused to sell the house and move to a lower-income neighborhood because status and friendships were more important. She became unhinged. We were all stressed and depressed, but she sought solace in prescription drugs.

There was a new pill that the Rolling Stones would later famously call "Mother's Little Helper." It was more commonly known as Valium, a powerful barbiturate used to treat anxiety disorders. My mother's brother-in-law was a doctor in Chicago, and he mailed her multiple bottles at a time. No one knew how highly addictive it was at the time, nor what it could do to your personality.

My mother quickly became dependent on Valium, and a six-months' supply would barely last her three. The bottle became a fixture on the kitchen counter, as common as a saltshaker.

Unfortunately, Valium only exacerbated my mother's condition, making her more depressed and even violent, especially with me. Verbal, emotional, and physical abuse became a daily routine.

On far too many occasions I was told how she never wanted to have me in the first place. I was an abomination. I was Satan's son. She was forced to have me because the devil wanted someone to carry his name.

She threatened to send me to the orphanage down the street, and regularly cornered me in my room until I was crying uncontrollably, curled up in a ball. This was not a healthy environment for an eight-year-old who had just lost his dad.

Only my guitar and memories of my father sustained me in my darkest hours back then. I did not forget that I used to mean something to someone; I had been the apple of my father's eye.

His love is the reason I defied gravity and survived the toxic trauma that soon became my life. His love was my salvation, yet the source of my sisters' pain.

It was not until fifty years later that I would discover how this childhood experience impacted many aspects of my life.

Boarding School, 1969

Chapter 4

From One Hell to Another

After my father died, everything in my life went to hell in a hand-basket. My mother's addiction and depression quickly found an outlet in me, and between 1965 and 1969, when I was left with my mother and two older sisters, life was a nightmare. They made me pay the price for all the years they were mistreated and neglected by my father. No child should ever have to carry that burden.

The elementary school I was attending in San Juan stopped at sixth grade, and there were three main middle and high schools that most of the boys in my class were applying to get into. All three schools were Catholic prep schools.

There was a fourth option that none of my friends were applying for: a remote, Catholic monastery with an all-boys boarding school, located in the mountains of Puerto Rico.

The fact that the school was far away made it seem like a distant, if foreboding, sanctuary.

The school had a reputation for being a kind of educational jail for delinquents. The only upside was that it had a great sports program, which I saw as another potential outlet for my emotional turmoil.

It was also known for being a very tough school academically, and the kids who graduated from there were seeing much higher acceptance rates at U.S. colleges than those graduating from other schools on the island. This didn't have the same appeal to me as the sports program, but I liked that the school would be laying the groundwork for my educational future. My dad had gone to MIT, and I felt that if I wanted to follow in his footsteps, I would need to get into a good college as well.

All of these things drew me to that school, but my main incentive was to leave my home life, which was getting progressively worse. I had to get out of there, so I applied to the boarding school, but also sent applications to the Catholic prep schools as a back-up.

I passed my entrance exams and got accepted into all four schools, so I clearly wasn't born with any learning disabilities. The cumulative effects of trauma, however, would later backfire.

Leaving home for boarding school seemed like a good decision, at least during the first two weeks. I loved everything about the place, and I felt far enough away from my angry sisters and crazy, violent mother.

In her agonizing depression, my mother barely kept food in the house, and she almost never cooked for us. The school, on the other hand, had an abundance of food.

The sports programs were as good as I had hoped, and I joined both the football and baseball teams.

But while my new school offered comfort, camaraderie, and fun, it also held a dark secret, something that would exacerbate the trauma I'd already experienced.

All the kids from the same grade had their lockers and slept in a common area. Each grade of roughly a hundred kids had their own floor.

It was here, on the cusp of adolescence, that I learned about the horror of what human beings could consciously inflict upon one another.

This all-boy boarding school run by Catholic, primarily German, Nazi-like priests, in a remote location in the countryside, was an all-too-perfect setting for bad things to happen. Very bad things.

We were all required to take these collective showers after playing sports. We would then go back to our official locker rooms to change, head to dinner, and attend our compulsory study hall period.

I never felt comfortable with the whole collective shower idea, but it was something I learned to get used to. Specifically, I got used to the fact that all you needed to do was mind your own business. Get in, get out. Period.

One of my very best friends, a twelve-year-old named Robert, was being harassed by the other boys in the shower one day. It was nothing serious, as far as I could tell, just the typical horsing around.

They were teasing Robert about how pretty he was. Robert was movie-star handsome. He had fine features with blond, almost white hair, and the bluest eyes you can imagine. The kids in the shower harassed Robert about how he was as pretty as his sisters, who themselves looked like models in a magazine.

I used to hang out with Robert on the weekends. He was happy to have someone around who wasn't going to harass him, and I was more than happy to be in close proximity to his pretty sisters. But the boys in the shower were talking about fucking Robert just like they wanted to fuck his sisters.

I didn't pay much attention to the teasing in the shower that day because it didn't look or sound more dangerous than the kind of restless bullying that regularly occurs between boys. I simply went about my business, left the showers, and walked towards the common locker room area.

A few minutes later, Robert ran into the locker room completely naked. He had sprinted from the shower stalls to the locker room, down three flights of stairs and halfway across the school, without so much as a towel.

He looked terrified.

A few seconds later, a group of five, much tougher, older kids followed him in, and they locked the door behind them, something that was expressly forbidden.

There were a few other seventh-graders in the locker room with me, but all of us quickly faded into the background.

The next thing I saw was these five guys wrestling Robert to the ground, holding him down, and raping him right in front of us. One of the older boys paused to make it perfectly clear that if anybody interfered, or if anybody talked, we would be next. In a matter of minutes that felt like forever, it was over.

Robert didn't last another week at that school. I was traumatized for him, and quite honestly, for myself. At twelve, I wasn't sure how to process what had happened. I didn't intervene or even try because I didn't want to be next. The possibility of saving Robert didn't measure up to my instinct for callous self-preservation.

And just as quickly as everything else had changed at every other stage of my life, school morphed into a terrifying prison of sorts.

My first personal encounter with sexual abuse was later that same year. The abuser wasn't another student, however, but one of God's chosen flock: a priest. The same one who called on others to confess their sins. The same one who administered the sacrament of "the body of Christ."

Father John was my Spanish teacher. And reading eighteenth-century Spanish literature was like putting needles in my eyeballs; I was not a good student in his class. In what I felt was a reasonable response to the dreariness of the subject matter, I horsed around endlessly, mocking Father John behind his back.

One day, Father John summoned me to the chapel after class while the other kids were running off to the sporting fields. I assumed he was going to make me pray away my rebelliousness and disruptive behavior. But once I got there, he asked me to follow him behind the chapel into the smaller, closed-door chapel.

In my mind, if the church was a holy sanctuary, this must have been an even holier place. I never suspected I was in harm's way.

Once we were alone in the chapel, Father John told me I was a very bad boy. He got right in my face and started to unbutton my shirt while rubbing my behind. He kissed me on the neck and touched me all over.

He wasn't planning on stopping there, and I didn't know what to make of this other than that nothing good was going on. My head felt light, and my thoughts were muddled, but I understood things just enough to sense where they were going. For a moment, at least, I gained enough clarity to fight back.

I pushed Father John away from me as hard as I could. He fell against the altar behind him, and everything crashed to the ground in a loud commotion. He looked at me like I was insane. How dare I push him like that? He screamed at me not to try walking away and that our discussion wasn't over.

Well, it was over for me.

I composed myself, buttoned my shirt, and bolted all the way to the sporting fields. Everybody was in their shorts and T-shirts playing sports. I was standing there in my school uniform, all sweaty and panting from having sprinted for what seemed like ten miles.

I wasn't going to let Father John get away with what he had done. Although I continued to go to class every day as was expected, I never did any of the homework. And during exams, I simply wrote my name at the top of the paper and handed it back to him. I got a 'B' in the class.

Years later I learned that the Catholic church had covered for many of these pedophillic priests.

When I told my mother about the incident and about what happened to Robert, she accused me of making the whole thing up.

"You are the worst human being ever born," she screamed at me. "You are not just the son of the devil, you are the devil himself!"

I wanted to switch schools, but she ordered me right back to that terror. She told me I had to apologize to Father John and to the other priests, but I refused. Luckily, she let that go, but there was no question I was going back to that hell to face whatever was next.

The short version is that this school was fertile ground for not only pedophiles, but every variety of sadistic child abuse you can imagine, all masked by the church.

A couple of the priests routinely hit our bare butts with a belt. Their preferred time for the belt beatings was at night. I remember too many of those beatings, hit by priests who reeked of rum and cigarettes. They were actually getting off on touching us, hitting us, abusing us. It was the kind of experience that changes your view of humanity.

There was one particular brother we called "El Demonio" (The Demon), because he was so cruel. Brother James was the mathematics teacher who doubled as the nighttime attendant for the ninth and tenth graders. James loved to wake us up in the middle of the night, physically yank us out of bed, and make us do exercises because he had supposedly heard noises coming from our room.

He would make us run laps around the football field at three a.m. in our PJ's or underwear, barefoot, for what seemed like hours. When he was really drunk, he would wake us up to do push-ups until we collapsed. I remember not being able to do any more push-ups, and he kicked me in the ribcage and said "Del Cueto, get back up and keep going. You are nowhere near done!"

This priest, a supposed man of God, seemed to enjoy this abuse more than anything else. He was a monster. He knew that forced push-ups would leave no visible abuse marks on our bodies, so there would never be any visible evidence.

Some students invented protest songs denouncing the insanity of the school to the tunes of the Beatles or the Rolling Stones. I would play the guitar as we sang, and it felt good to rebel.

By gathering together in our free moments, we were making it harder for these sadist pedophiles to have their way with us. There was strength in numbers. We saw it as a simple outlet, but I think our innocent musical rebellion kept us safe. I was class president for a few years, but it was my guitar that taught me the real potential of leadership.

Before the last day of the ninth grade, we decided to mess with Brother James when he came for us in the middle of the night.

We planned to make more than enough noise to wake him up from his usual drunken stupor, and when he'd turn on the lights and try to yank us out of bed, we wouldn't complain that it was the middle of the night or that we were tired, we would do the opposite.

So when "El Demonio" burst into our room that night, we immediately started clapping and talking it up as if we were at football practice. The team captain took over and we started doing our own set of routines on his command: push-ups, sit-ups, and jumping jacks, before Brother James could get a word in.

We were in control, not him.

Brother James was furious. He was screaming for us to stop and follow his commands, but we wouldn't listen. We just got louder and louder. He even tried to belt a couple of kids, and that's when the bigger boys pushed him to the side. He threw punches at a couple of us, so we shoved him until he fell to the ground.

There were over a hundred of us fourteen-year-olds against one drunk, middle-aged priest, and we were finally fighting back.

It felt great to watch him run out of the room, stripped of his power. But then the school principal, Father Juan, stormed in and smashed a baseball bat against one of the columns in our dorm room. Splinters from the bat flew everywhere, and we got the point. He threatened to flunk each one of us if we did not behave. This priest meant business.

I spent four-and-a-half years in that prison... I mean school, during which one kid had his head slammed into the desk so hard that he suffered a concussion. Another kid had his head smashed through a window and had to be rushed to the hospital. Way too many of my classmates simply disappeared, never to be seen or heard from again. The characters who were supposed to be taking care of us were more dangerous than convicts in an actual jail, and it feels good to finally talk about what we all went through.

Years later I met with another classmate at a school luncheon in Miami, and learned for certain that I was not alone. He was the first person I met who spoke of experiences similar to my own. He told me to Google some of the priests who had been our caretakers, and it turns out that many of them were finally being expelled from the church, and were even the subjects of multiple lawsuits.

I wasn't just making this up, nor did I simply have a hyper-active imagination. The horror was real. I was part of the humongous dark cloud of child abuse and pedophilia that hangs over the Roman Catholic Church and other religious institutions. I'm just grateful to have lived to tell the tale.

I have not talked publicly about my abuse, but I pray for other children whose lives are forever destroyed under the guise of religion. No God that I know would ever approve of His church being used for such atrocities.

Today we know that most abusers were abused themselves, and that they can't help but repeat the pattern. It's almost too much to comprehend.

I am now what I call a "Recovering Catholic." I embrace Christian theology in principle, but I refuse to attend an actual church for mass or any other reason.

What happened behind those walls turned me away from organized religion, but it did not take away my faith in God.

The school eventually opened its doors to students from a neighboring co-ed Catholic school, and things got a little better. Even a bunch of abused teenagers couldn't help but find hope in seeing that girls were finally allowed in that school for the first time in its twenty-five years. I think it was a PR move to try and soften the "jail-like" image that the school had in Puerto Rico at the time.

Things started looking up for me on a personal level as well. A family that recently moved to the island from Oklahoma, the Minnicks, saved my life by inviting me to live with them. I will forever appreciate and remember their generosity.

But in 1974, in the middle of my junior year, after I had already ordered my high school graduation ring, I was expelled for being part of a school-wide prank: we stole the football team's jerseys the night before their first game of the season. I think the school was looking for an excuse to get rid of me, and that was as good a reason as any.

The Minnick family was transferring back to the U.S. so the school sent me back to my mother, who had become a full-blown addict by this point, and I quickly lost hope that life at home would ever be normal.

With my guitar, 1974

Chapter 5

Survival: Starving Teen to Entrepreneur

Baldwin High School was a local branch of a famous liberal arts school in New York City. It catered to the sons and daughters of the American executives living in Puerto Rico. It was a hippie school with loose policies; the opposite of where I was coming from.

The administration agreed to accept me in the middle of the school year if I committed to playing sports every semester. From my first days in the new school I thought I had died and gone to heaven: there were no uniforms, and the class sizes were tiny.

Almost all the kids were from rich families, and pretty, bra-less girls with liberal values and attitudes were everywhere. It was an American movie come true. On my first day of school I was shocked to find a group of boys and girls smoking weed in the bathroom.

As an athlete and guitar player, I didn't have much trouble making new friends. I was a big fish in a small pond. A handful of kids and I formed a band, and we got to play at school parties. Being the lead guitarist in a band didn't hurt with the girls, either.

Having come from such a strict educational system, this new environment felt like a breeze, and I was actually getting good grades without even trying. I finally felt comfortable in my own skin; people actually liked me for me.

Later they also liked me for having the best weed, but when I first joined that high school I didn't even smoke pot, much less sell it. In fact, I still hated drugs because they reminded me of everything that was wrong with my mother.

But the situation at home was grim. I was willing to do whatever it took to survive, so I started selling pot to make ends meet. I was just a scared, sixteen-year-old kid with illegal substances in my guitar case, transporting them in my car. But running drugs on a small scale proved easy, and I quickly learned that "business" was in my blood.

Unfortunately, this also led to my own addictions down the road. Memories of my mother's drug habit were initially enough to keep me clean, but drugs ultimately became my own way of coping with the nightmare of home.

Mother was living alone (she didn't re-marry), and her drug dependency worsened. People suspected that something was wrong with her, but nobody understood what was going on; they just thought her difficult circumstances and terror of a son were too much to bear, so she maintained her status as the neighborhood saint.

I was a teenager living with a junkie who wanted to kill me, but in everyone's eyes, she could do no wrong.

She still kept no food at the house so I was left to fend for myself. I needed to play sports every afternoon to keep my scholarship, but I also needed lunch money and gas money for the old car that she let me use to drive myself to school.

A band-mate told me that a few students had been expelled for selling weed on campus. One of those guys was Chuck, who was a terrible guitar player but an excellent pot dealer. Luckily for me, Chuck wanted to improve his guitar-playing skills, and he was always inviting me to his house so I could teach him some new licks.

I noticed the enormous amount of weed in his closet, and asked what had happened to his customers at the high school.

"They're all still there," he said. "But I'm not allowed on campus anymore. They'll either find a way to get here, or they'll find another pot dealer."

Stop the presses! The weed is here and the hungry customers are at my school. I can be the go-between and transport just enough to make the money I needed for gas and food. My teenage mind did not fully understand the consequences.

"How hard can this be?" I rationalized. "How dangerous can this get?"

At first I was only transporting very small amounts. It made me nervous because I had to carry the guitar case from Chuck's house to mine and all around school. I even opened it to play guitar between classes to keep up appearances.

I knew that my mother would never bail me out if the cops caught me, and a prison cell in Puerto Rico for a sixteen-year-old boy wasn't very appealing. But as time went on, I started transporting bigger quantities and consuming my own product.

This was the beginning of my personal drug abuse, which would later become a debilitating substance addiction. It was also the beginning of my addiction to the high-risk, high-reward world of drug distribution.

I am not proud of this time in my life. I knew that I had crossed a couple of lines, but no teenager should have to hustle drugs in order to eat.

I developed a pattern of leaving the house early in the morning each day, and then coming home after practice to quickly shower and change before my mother got home from work to avoid seeing her.

As you can imagine, nothing good came from being driven to the streets every evening. I got and stayed high all night, and then used those nighttime hours to expand my clientele, hanging around a tougher crowd.

It wasn't long before I met Chuck's pot connection, who happened to be the older brother of another high school friend. This friend was extremely wealthy, and his brother was the primary marijuana importer in Puerto Rico in the mid-seventies.

I went from filling my closet with weed to renting entire houses just for storage. I was no longer in the small-time retail pot business of selling baggies to the rich kids in my school, I was distributing mass quantities in wholesale to all kinds of people across San Juan.

Even as I found grittier and grittier people to associate with, I continued telling myself that this was all temporary. My plan was still to leave Puerto Rico as soon as I graduate from high school. My life goal was to become a rock star.

After high school I moved to Miami, Florida to pursue my dreams of stardom, but what I found was one of the most dangerous places in the world for a desperate teenager with a drug problem.

Up to no good, 1970's

Chapter 6

College and Capitalism

After barely making it out of high school in Puerto Rico, I left for Miami at seventeen, just as I'd planned.

My best friend's dad had purchased a brand-new condo for him across the street from a community college, and they offered me a guest bedroom at no charge because I had nowhere else to go.

Still dreaming of being a rock-star, I registered as a music major at the local community college. Unfortunately, even though I could play music by ear, I couldn't read music sheets to save my life. No matter how hard I tried, the notes looked like incomprehensible spaghetti.

A music theory professor tried to help me. He took me aside and asked if I had the focus and discipline to practice eight hours a day. "If not," he said, "then a music degree is probably a bad choice for you, and a complete waste of everyone's time."

Normally I took remarks like that as a challenge to prove people wrong, but in this case I knew he was probably right.

I walked back to my apartment kicking every little pebble along the way. What would I tell people? That my plan had failed? I had no plan B, and I felt like my future had been blown to bits. So I went to my room and put my guitar away.

This marked the start of a race to the bottom, and the beginning of the five darkest years of my life.

As you might have seen in the films *Cocaine Cowboys* or *Scarface*, Miami in 1975 was not exactly a safe place for a lost teenager whose life plan had just been nuked. I was living side-by-side with the people who inspired those movies. I can look back now and say there was nothing sexy about it.

The combination of all the dangerous elements in South Florida in those days was highly combustible. The Vietnam War was over, but it left legions of young veterans in its wake, returning home traumatized, highly proficient with guns, and all-too-comfortable with serious violence. The GI bill may have helped some of them get back to school and feed themselves, but it couldn't make them whole again.

Miami was full of its own distinct flavors of organized crime: there were the Cuban kids with their junior syndicates of sort; there were the kids from New York and New Jersey, many of whom had "uncles" and older brothers who were a part of the real, Sopranos-style Italian mafia; there was the Jewish mob; and of course, the South American gangs, who were the ultimate drug connection.

Add the local Southerners to the mix, and you've got a whole lot of "bad hombres" who know how to navigate the dirt roads, the backwaters in the Keys, the Everglades, and the swamps. They helped all the other organizations gain their foothold in the territory.

Many representatives from these groups saw the community college and its surrounding neighborhoods as ideal markets for their product, so it didn't take me long to make friends with these individuals. I certainly had experience in the industry, but it also made me numb to its risks. After all, my plan to study music had blown up in my face, and I still needed a way to make ends meet.

The next eighteen months are kind of a haze for me. My habitual pot smoking quickly escalated to harder drugs, and the more entangled I became with the distribution side of the business, the more I consumed their products in larger quantities.

Here's how the drug trade worked in Miami: the Cuban mafia focused on cocaine. They were importing it and then selling it locally

The Italians were the marijuana importers, moving large shipments from Colombia and Jamaica. They would bring it in but send it directly to the Northeast U.S. by car. They never bothered distributing to the local market.

Then there were the Jews, who were into the barbiturates and the opioids. They were working in the opposite direction, bringing Quaaludes and opioids down from the Northeast U.S., and distributing them locally in South Florida.

So I started selling the Italians' pot to the Cubans, and the Cubans' coke to the Italians. Talk about commerce! And since everybody wanted the Jews' products, I distributed the barbiturates to both the Italians and the Cubans.

Business was booming and life was good. I was popular and had lots of cash, so I spent much of my time in Miami's disco scene, going out to the clubs almost every night of the week. I was learning the basics of capitalism, even if the specifics were a little unconventional. It was not the college education I had in mind, but who needs business school when you can learn about trade, supply, demand, and how to play the market while having a grand old time?

Unfortunately, this lifestyle didn't include logic or safety, especially when it came to driving. One evening a group of us was heading out, and since I appeared to be the in the best shape to drive, I popped a couple of downers (Quaaludes) before getting in the car, and their effect hit me as soon as I merged onto the highway. I was going seventy miles per hour when all of a sudden I had blurry, double vision. It's a miracle I didn't crash and die that night along with everyone else in the car.

Quaaludes had become a daily fix to numb myself from life's cruel realities. Like my mother, I became a full-blown pill junkie. The apple didn't fall far from that tree.

I needed help, and I had to rely on others to shake me out of this fog. One of my suppliers, Reuben, a nice Jewish boy from New York, summoned a group of us to his apartment, where I'd attended numerous parties over the last several months.

"We're all addicted to the Quaaludes," he declared. "And we are all going to stop. We are to never see each other again; we need to go get cleaned-up on our own."

The next two weeks were miserable. Barbiturate addiction is every bit as painful to kick as a heroin problem.

There I was, an eighteen-year-old kid in Miami with no direction, no health insurance, and no rehab facility to help me cope with withdrawals. I had to do this on my own.

I told myself that I had made the choice to get into this terrible situation in the first place, so it was up to me to get myself out. I was sick for days. It was one of the lowest points of my life, but I did it. I survived the detox, and lived to fight another day.

Meanwhile, the drug trade was steaming right along. My mafia friends from New York, Cuba, and Colombia were getting bolder, and violence was starting to creep in.

Up until that point, my drug-running friends had kept the guns in the background. There were always guns in the houses, but they were just there as a precautionary measure. Now, a different crowd was starting to show up at my friends' houses, and they took pride in their weapons.

It became more difficult to convince myself that this was all harmless when I'd have to make room on a table full of weapons just to roll a joint. And these weren't your run-of-the-mill handguns, they were submachine guns and pistols with silencers; weapons for those with more than self-defense in mind.

Something was definitely shifting, particularly among my Cuban friends, who seemed more paranoid than the rest.

Anton, for example, was a young man with whom I had done plenty of business. He was one of my Cuban mafia friends. We were hanging out at his mom's house one day, in a quiet, lower middle-class, Cuban neighborhood in Miami (talk about low key! This man was moving kilos of pure Colombian coke while his mother offered us snacks), when Anton told me, "Things are changing and getting more violent, Joe. I need to make sure you can defend yourself if need be."

He proceeded to show me how to make a homemade bomb that could blow up a car with a simple combination of drain cleaner, crystals, plastic baggies, duct-tape, and some rubber bands.

"If someone ever messes with you, just use this to blow up their car," he said. "The only problem is that it's a simple time-release device, so there's no way to know who will be in the car when it blows up."

Anton's intentions were noble: he just wanted to protect me now that Miami was turning more violent. Although I wasn't a perfect kid by any measure, my moral compass wouldn't tilt this far. I wasn't about to blow up anyone's car, and I wasn't going to kill anyone, not even by mistake.

Sam, a young Puerto Rican buddy of mine, was the first of my friends to get arrested and go to federal prison. He ran with the Colombian crowd, selling coke in bulk. Sammy was always more reckless than most of us, determined to be "big-time," but he never understood the concept of staying low-key. He was released a few months after his incarceration, but gunned down on that same day. Shortly after that, I got a call from the FBI, asking me questions about Sammy. That was my tipping point. I was now on the FBI's radar; this had to be the end of the ride for me.

I made a quick but resolute decision to leave Miami for Gainesville, Florida, about four hours north, but a million times tamer.

It was a sleepy, little, college town with a hippie vibe, the hometown of rocker Tom Petty. I knew nothing about it other than some rumors that the locals grew some pristine marijuana.

The rumors were true. Gainesville had some wonderful home-grown weed, too good to be so cheap. My first weekend there was Halloween of 1976, and it was wonderful. I just wandered from one student party to another, having a blast, getting high, and getting laid. It was the routine to which I had grown accustomed, minus the piles of cocaine and the visible weapons. There were no apparent "bad guys" or mobster-types lurking amongst these kids. It seemed like the perfect escape from my criminal trajectory, so I began anew.

By January of 1977 I enrolled in the Santa Fe Community College, and got an apartment in Gainesville with a couple of friends. I was determined to make a serious pass at a college degree once again, this time without the distractions or reckless influences and heavy drugs.

An aptitude test pointed me towards advertising as a possible career. It seemed perfect for me as it combined the creativity I had once hoped to express through my music, and the sales skills I had learned on the streets.

The plan was to get my associates degree at Santa Fe, and then transfer to the University of Florida to get my bachelor's degree in advertising. I would pay for my studies with work-study programs and student loans like everybody else. I didn't need money for much else in this college town, where everything seemed cheap by comparison to Miami. My roommates both had cars, so I didn't even need my own transportation.

The first couple of semesters were okay, but I struggled in school and couldn't focus for reasons that I did not yet understand. Although pot quieted my mind and really helped me concentrate on homework, it did not stop me from making bad decisions.

One day, when I clearly wasn't thinking straight, I cashed my student loan check, stopped by a local drug dealer to score everything I could get, and spent an entire semester's worth of funds at Mardi Gras in New Orleans, getting drunk and high with a bunch of friends. I take full responsibility for this impulsive, reckless, and stupid ridiculousness.

Soon after my recklessness in the Big Easy, I was itching for more action. Gainesville was too slow for me. I wanted to get high on something much stronger than home-grown pot and beer like the rest of the students. I looked for the coke and Quaalude dealers, and they weren't hard to find.

Before long I was back to using hard drugs, but I managed to find some balance in Gainesville through exercise, of all things. It was a healthy town where everybody went to the gym, ran, or swam, and I found my way to jogging. I had played sports all through high school so I had a predisposition to running, even if it meant jogging while stoned out of my head. And that became my daily routine: go to class, get stoned, run 5 or 6 miles and work out, have dinner, get stoned, do homework/study, get stoned, repeat.

It certainly seemed to be a healthier and more sustainable model than I ever had in Miami. I smoked pot on weekdays, and saved the harder drugs for the weekend. Responsible, no?

I thought I could do it all, except I was struggling financially. It sucks to be poor when you know how to make easy money, albeit illegally.

I was determined to give this whole going-to-college thing a try without diving back into the drug business, but I needed some financial help.

During Christmas break that year, I went to Puerto Rico and asked my grandfather to finance my education. He was already in his late sixties, and he had moved to Puerto Rico with my grandmother to help their now-widowed, very sick daughter with her kids. I didn't exactly have a great track record, and I had the worst public relations agent in the world:

his daughter, my insane, junkie mother, who deeply resented my very existence. So the odds of him helping me weren't good.

My grandfather decided to give me a test period, but strictly under his terms: he hand-picked the hardest classes for me to take (accounting, business law, and chemistry), and he wanted me to take them as a full-time student in one semester. He would send me the exact funds for tuition, rent, and food.

I agreed to go along with anything he decided, as long as I didn't have to worry about paying the bills. I didn't want to resort to the drug business that I knew all too well.

None of my roommates or neighbors were taking the same classes, so I desperately needed transportation to get to and from school. So I decided to do the unthinkable: I sold my guitar. I traded my 1950s Gibson Les Paul Jr. that had been "my baby" and prized possession since high school for a motorcycle that'd take me back and forth to Santa Fe.

If I was going to make this college plan work, there was no room for any romanticized, wannabe rock-star ideas like owning a great, electric guitar that went untouched under my bed for months on end.

I paid attention in class and got good grades (even when I started dealing a little pot on the side for extra cash). I stayed on track and got all A's and one B.

At the end of the semester I headed back to Puerto Rico, hoping my grandfather would see my grades and continue supporting my college education at Santa Fe, and then at the University of Florida after that. But things didn't quite turn out the way I thought they would. My mother and other family members had apparently convinced him that I was a bad bet regardless of what proof I had to the contrary.

"If you want me to help you through college," he said, "you must attend Oral Roberts University in Oklahoma, where all of your cousins are going."

There was no way I was going to move to Oklahoma! I went back to Gainesville with broken dreams, again, but I wasn't ready to give up just yet. I was still determined to continue school, I just needed to replace my grandfather's allowance with another source of income.

I naturally defaulted to what I knew best: 'the biz.' I talked to some of my friends and neighbors, as well as a few dealers in town, and everybody pointed me in the same direction: the local pot growers.

As it turned out, the great home-grown pot I had been smoking for over a year was being manufactured by these really smart hippies who decided to live in the country and pursue legitimate farming and horticultural businesses, while growing "sinsemilla" (seedless marijuana) on the side.

It was a very disorganized group of people with some great product and enormous potential. I told one of the growers that I could expand his market and double his profits in a matter of weeks if only he'd give me enough product to take to Miami on consignment. I knew plenty of people over there who would pay good money for it.

After manicuring the scraggly-looking homemade buds, I packaged them in Mason jars and even gave them a name: "Gainesville Green." I priced them at a premium (about five times what these hippies were selling it for), and drove to Miami. I told the grower that I would double his profits, and I was going to keep my promise; I was just planning on making a little extra on the side for myself.

Gainesville Green became an instant sensation. The grower turned his entire crop over to me for distribution, and then introduced me to the other growers, with whom I quickly became well acquainted.

The months that followed were absolutely great. I had become the go-to guy for distribution, marketing, and other products like "Micanopy Madness," "Purple Haze," "Grower's Delight," and "Christmastime."

The buyers couldn't get enough of that Gainesville weed, and my finances improved considerably. I was rolling in dough again, but my studies were naturally starting to slip because I started using cocaine and Quaaludes on a daily basis again.

I didn't have the time or the head for school, so I dropped out once again, this time in the middle of my senior year as an advertising student.

The straw that broke the camel's back came when a friend who specialized in fixing horse races across the country asked me to grow some pot on his farm down in Ocala. I thought it would be a no-brainer gig, so I accepted the business proposition without hesitation.

After working with him for a while, he invited his son and I to go for a ride, and I figured we'd be scouting for another place to grow pot in the woods, which wasn't uncommon.

He stopped the truck in the middle of a dirt road in the Ocala National Forest, and told us both to get out. He hurdled a large boulder into a swamp on the side of the road and it slowly sank; it was quicksand. Without saying a word, his message was loud and clear: This is what happens to my enemies, get it?

I was back with the bad guys. Another scene from a terrible drug movie had just occurred in my life.

Later that same week he wanted to discuss the viability of assassinating one of my growers so we can take over his crop. I was right back in Miami circa 1975, except it was Central Florida five years later. I was rebuilding my own prison wherever I went.

I ran away from that farm in Ocala and never looked back. I just hunkered down in Gainesville, and hit the harder drugs more than ever before.

My new, full-time job was to mind one of my growers' fields when he fled the country in a hurry. I just hung around the farm right outside of town all day, wearing steel-reinforced boots because of the snakes, camouflage shorts, and a .45-caliber pistol stuffed in my back pocket. Stoned out of my mind, I spent most of the time paranoid that we were either going to be raided by some bad guys who wanted to kill us, or by drug enforcement agents, who were a relatively new threat in the area.

In the past, the local sheriffs had actually been our distribution partners. They'd deliver the stuff right out of their cruisers; it was unbelievable.

Now, times were changing.

The mellow, hippie, pot-dealing business was going the same route as the heyday of the drug trade in Miami. Even in Gainesville, the violent bad guys were moving in.

My personal life also took a sad turn when my college girlfriend left me, saying I had turned into a slime ball. She was probably right.

The very last week I was there, one of my closest friends, a fellow who sold drugs for the Jewish mob out of Jacksonville, invited me to a dinner party at his house. He had printed invitations and demanded that we RSVP. More importantly, he demanded that we all show up on time. I found this rather unusual, as we were all a bunch of rather loose characters; we didn't do anything with that kind of formality.

"Do you have any idea what's going on with Josh?" I asked another friend.

"He invited twelve of us to his house for dinner; no dates allowed," he replied. "He is in serious debt to his mob bosses in Jacksonville, so he is going to blow his brains out at the dinner table. This is his 'last supper.'"

That was it for me. I knew I was done.

I decided to run as fast and as far as I could from all this insanity, so I ran to the only place I could think of: all the way back to Puerto Rico, back to my crazy mother's house.

And of all places in the world, it was there that I found what saved me.

Cyndi, my angel

Chapter 7

Finding Cynthia; My Angel

When I called my mother to tell her I was in trouble and wanted to come home, she was surprisingly compassionate.

"Get on a plane and come to Puerto Rico," she urged me. "Just leave everything behind; none of it matters. Just get out of there!"

I left a fully-furnished apartment with a closet full of clothes behind, and had a good friend drive me to the airport. We ceremoniously burnt my "little black book" in the parking lot, setting fire to all of the names and phone numbers of my drug connections and customers so I wouldn't be tempted to look back.

What awaited me back in Puerto Rico was a mother with a growing addiction to barbiturates, opioids, and other prescription drugs that she'd been using for more than five years. It wasn't long before I became the target of her unstable emotional and mental breakdowns once again.

She made it a point to sabotage my job seeking efforts with various advertising firms on the island by telling them I was a no-good drug dealer.

Her circle of influence was pretty wide. She was admired by the people in our community as a high school typing teacher, widowed before she was forty, never remarried, a devout Catholic who went to church every Sunday, and raised three kids all by herself.

To the outside world this woman was a saint. No one knew about the junkie, sick monster I knew.

Our lowest point together was the evening she came at me with a butcher's knife during one of her outbreaks. She took a couple of swipes at me, and although I managed to wrestle the knife out of her hand, I was badly cut in the process.

Bleeding profusely with a big gash in my right hand, I ran to my best friend's house with my hand wrapped in a T-shirt. I needed multiple stitches and a shot of penicillin.

The same grandfather who demanded I move to Oklahoma came over to my mother's house that night and asked me to pack my clothes. I was going to live with him and my grandmother in a much poorer, but surprisingly safer, part of town; away from my mother.

My grandmother, however, did not care for this idea at all. She, like my mother, saw me as the spitting image of my father. My looks, swagger, and charisma, were all reminders of the man who had neglected her daughter and granddaughters.

Helpful as ever, my grandfather bought me a cheap car so I could get around the island, but my grandmother refused to feed me. Her reasoning was that I'd be more likely to get a job and move out of her house if I was uncomfortable. She didn't want me there in the first place, so she certainly wasn't going to make it easy for me to stay.

Behind my grandmother's back, my grandfather would generously slip me food; a gesture I am still thankful for in my daily prayers. He used to sit and watch me workout every day. He seemed to appreciate that I was trying to exorcise my demons and kick my drug dependencies through sheer determination and physical exertion.

I managed to get an entry-level clerk position at an ad agency owned by a friend's neighbor. Years later, when I opened a Puerto Rico branch of my own business, I ended up buying that same agency.

As much as my early life had been difficult, and as much as my quest for real love ended when my father passed away, God brought someone into my life who became my whole world.

One night, while visiting my friend Bobby at his mother's house, this cute, twenty-year-old girl with the best smile in the world was there. It was love at first sight, which I didn't believe was possible until that moment.

I found myself talking to this beautiful, single mom into the wee hours of the night. I was completely enamored with this woman. There was something about her, maybe the fact that she was a little broken herself? Getting pregnant at barely eighteen and keeping the baby must have taken a lot of courage, especially as the relationship with the baby's father dissolved. She was traveling through life with her child, without a real home or parents to speak of.

Cindy closed the deal for eternity with me when I told her about getting dumped by my college girlfriend. She looked at me and said, "But you have so much potential."

I was stunned that someone saw my potential. It was like she saw straight to my soul. We got a small place for the three of us, and we both worked every day to get by.

Cindy and I soon decided to get married. Well, technically, she gave me an ultimatum: she didn't want her child's heart to be broken by more disappearing fathers, so we were to either get married or part ways. We had a small wedding by the pool in our apartment building because there was no money for anything else, but we were very happy.

My life was starting to find a sense of balance and stability. My transition from drug dealer to a married father was immediate and final.

I had turned a corner. I made a commitment to Cindy and to myself to never sell drugs again. I still used them recreationally until my second daughter was born a few years later, but I never sold again.

Cindy was my guardian angel. She had saved my life. She was ready, willing, and able to urge me towards the success she believed I could have.

I now think of my life in two parts: LBC (Life Before Cindy), and LAC (Life After Cindy). This woman continues to mean the world to me.

After Cindy and I got married, my life was blessed in other ways as well. I was making headway in the advertising field after working for a couple of ad agencies, and I even opened a small promotions company that did extremely well.

Then I got one of the best advertising jobs available in Puerto Rico at a marketing company. Things were going well until Cindy and I discovered that the owner was cheating us out of some commissions.

Cindy walked into my office one day and started taking the pictures off the walls and putting them in boxes. In her simple but powerful way she said, "We are getting you out of here. There is no need to have this place rip us off. We are leaving right now."

It was tough leaving that job because it was the most money I had ever legally made.

Trying to think of other business opportunities, I figured that since I couldn't be a musician, I might as well do the next best thing and become a music promoter. But this was not a great idea.

Making the connections with musicians and their booking agents in the U.S. proved more difficult than I thought it would be. I didn't have those connections, and they weren't easy to make.

Cindy and I struggled financially for the next couple of years. She was the breadwinner, working as an assistant in a law firm, and I tried getting different ideas off the ground.

When Cindy became pregnant with our second daughter, Cristina, we were absolutely elated that our family was expanding, but our financial situation kept getting worse.

We were so financially strapped by the time Cristina was born that we had to sell everything: our car, furniture, and even our bed, just to pay for the hospital where our daughter was to be born. We couldn't pay rent or cover the daycare tuition for the school where our now four-year-old daughter, Paola, was going. Fortunately, both our landlord and the head of the school were extremely understanding. I will never forget their generosity.

It was a difficult time. But perhaps the best lesson was that we didn't let our struggle tear us apart.

I kept reading advertising and media magazines, and there was a growing Spanish-speaking population in the U.S., and an entirely new industry was quickly forming around it.

Cindy suggested that we move to the U.S. so I can pursue a job in this growing Hispanic market. She said I would be perfect for it.

We were an inch away from being homeless with a 4-year-old and a newborn baby.

Cindy's grandparents, who raised her, lived in the Puerto Rican countryside in a cinder-block home that was partially built by her grandfather. They were barely surviving themselves, so we couldn't ask them for help. And my family was definitely out of the question, so our backs were against the wall.

We devised a plan: I was to leave for the U.S. without them while she and the girls would move-in with her grandparents until I get settled with a job. Leaving my family behind, with my newborn baby girl in the Puerto Rican countryside was heartbreaking.

On July 10, 1984, I got on a plane and left Puerto Rico to look for a better future for my family.

I went to Orlando, Florida to stay with a childhood friend who had a townhouse where I could stay while looking for a job. Orlando was somewhat familiar to me. I had been a Disney tour guide for a while back in college, and there were now quite a few Puerto Ricans living there. Perhaps, I thought, I would find the U.S. Hispanic market that I was looking for in Orlando.

And then it dawned on me: I AM the U.S. Hispanic market!

Chapter 8

Miami-Bound for a New Life

In search of the American dream, I pledged to find my fortunes in a new land, and to do it legally.

After two weeks of unsuccessful job interviews in Orlando, I bought a clunky, used car for three-hundred-bucks, and drove it to my aunt and uncle's house in Miami. They had not only agreed to let me stay with them, but to also host Cindy and the kids as soon as I landed a full-time job.

My first job in Miami was at Arregui Advertising. My wife and the children arrived, but my aunt, a raging alcoholic, immediately hated Cindy with a passion. This fragile arrangement did not last very long; we were kicked out after only a couple of months.

Another ad agency in Fort Lauderdale hired me next, but the hour-and-a-half commute in each direction was too much for my clunker of a car. That's when we moved to Miramar, a town closer to my work, and Cindy decided to also get a job. We eventually settled into a good routine.

As luck would have it, I met a wonderful, kind-hearted salesman from a start-up Spanish-language TV network, who told me I was wasting my talents working at the ad agency.

"The money is in Spanish-language TV," he asserted. But what did I know about TV? I only knew advertising, sales promotion, and marketing, yet he insisted on setting up a meeting with the network executives, so I went.

I immediately hit it off with Blaine, my soon-to-be new boss, who recently moved from New York City to start the network in Florida. He gave me my first break in the business.

It was the Miami affiliate of a Spanish-language TV network. They initially hired me as an entry-level clerk, but I was quickly promoted and started traveling around the country to convince companies to advertise on Spanish-language TV in order to reach the growing Hispanic population.

I had finally found something that really fit.

Chapter 9

Getting My Foundation in Business

Timing is everything, and my entrance into this sector coincided with an explosive growth of the Hispanic market.

My career at Univision and Telemundo was in the national sales and marketing department. I traveled to our headquarters in New York City on a weekly basis, and frequently visited Los Angeles, San Francisco, Dallas, and Chicago.

I loved the energy of travel, seeing new places, and interacting with people at the highest level. I came into my own as I learned to sell, engage, and lead. This was a time of great growth for my confidence in my ability to be successful.

My job was to talk to the big, national companies about the growing Hispanic market that was now living across the U.S., and how they were missing out on selling their goods and services to this huge community. My message was simple but controversial: if they didn't advertise in Spanish on Spanish TV, they were not connecting with an audience that was already in place and growing.

"Why can't they all learn English?" My clients would ask. It was hard to hear, but that was the reality.

The shift in demographics faced plenty of push-back, but eventually caught on. I became the Vice President of Domestic Productions by the time I was thirty years old, and ran the entire sales and marketing operations for Telemundo in New York City by thirty-two.

Cindy and I had a baby boy and two little girls who loved to be around me, but I was constantly traveling. A happy home-life eluded me, just as it had since I was a small boy.

In 1994 I was approached by a Latin American media owner. He was a billionaire who recently won the rights to a few television stations in a court settlement. Since he wasn't an American citizen, he asked that I keep the TV stations he won, and send his family a percentage of the revenue.

Doing this would require me to move to Orlando, and I wasn't about to do that. Our working relationship took a downturn, and he wanted out. He said I could keep the business if I wanted to, and repay his initial investment whenever I could.

I was scared to death, but I decided to take the risk, which turned out to be a good thing because the business quickly boomed. We opened offices in San Juan, Puerto Rico, and Mexico City.

It all seemed promising until the dot-com era emerged in the late-nineties. Miami became ground zero for all Latin American dot-com companies. The San Francisco Bay Area had Silivon Valley, New York City had Silicon Alley, and Miami had Silicon Beach.

I got myself deeply entangled in the Spanish dot-coms, and we all thought we were going to be multi-millionaires. We were raising money on Wall Street, hanging around the top investment houses in the country -sometimes the world- who were all catering to us with the intention to help us go public in the near future. At least that was the plan.

Surrounded by CEOs, we were smoking Cuban cigars and counting our chickens before they hatched. Just a bunch of young men pretending we were going to be gazillionaries. We had paper and stock options, and we were trading them like kids used to trade baseball cards. My wife, watching all of us from afar, knew how foolish this was. "You can't take these stock options to the grocery store," she would say, but I wasn't hearing any of it. We were enamored with ourselves.

All of our dreams went up in smoke when the dot-com bubble burst in 2000. Many of these companies went out of business. We simply ran out of cash and folded. There were no bankruptcies, we were just forced to stop operations.

This sparked my second breakdown.

At Univision, 1993

Chapter 10

Invincible, Until I Wasn't

I received a severance package generous enough to launch my own company. Cindy wasn't going to sit on the sidelines and watch me crash again, so she became the Chief Financial Officer, my 50/50 partner.

Trying to make ends meet again, I was selling myself as a consultant, hiring myself out for random projects to pay the bills.

I became depressed. We had one kid coming out of college, another in high school, and the youngest in middle school. We had some savings and a good amount of home equity, but I invested the majority of our cash in the company.

I'd never seen a mental health professional before. After a bad reaction to the antidepressants that my regular doctor prescribed, I saw a credible psychiatrist who looked at me and said, "Joe, you're broken. But don't worry; I can fix you."

I couldn't pay, so he worked on consignment.

He set me on a better path, and rewired my central nervous system. Just as you'd a fix broken toy, he started putting me back together.

I picked myself up and got a lucky break from a New York-based Hispanic ad agency. "We're going after a global pharmaceutical company. You do media, we do creative. But you fund your own pitch trip."

We got to Philadelphia, where a high school buddy of mine from boarding school was sitting at the head of the table, and I was hired on the spot.

I contacted an agency with an office on Madison Avenue and another in Beverly Hills to form an alliance. The CEO introduced me to his partners, and just as he was about to introduce me to another he said, "The guy you're about to meet is a piece of work. Some of his stories are so amazing that they are hard to believe. I've been trying to catch him in a lie for the past twenty years. His stuff is out of the movies."

It was my seventh grade English teacher, but not one of the priests; he was a good guy from my days in Puerto Rico. He was working as a partner at the agency, and has evidently had a tremendous career.

He took me under his wing, taught me the new performance model, and I was instantly in love.

Chapter 11

The Comeback Kid

Business is as much about reacting to failure as it is about dealing with success. It's a cliché that can be hard to grasp until you've felt it hammered home. Those who are successful are the ones who know how to get back up after they fall. They deal with the loss and move forward. This mindset has served me well.

After several failed attempts to build sustainable and scalable businesses, I finally discovered Direct Marketing; not a sexy business by any definition, but what everyone does to generate sales and revenue. It's the least glamorous part of advertising and branding.

Even though the U.S. Hispanic market was now a multi-billion-dollar industry, it was 2006, and the U.S. economy was showing signs of trouble. Advertisers were becoming increasingly careful and apprehensive about their marketing investments, now that Google had introduced a pay-for-performance model of engagement with clients. Advertisers started demanding return on investment (ROI) marketing.

What was needed in the Hispanic market was accountability and results. I met with a Cable TV executive who looked at me and said, "If you can pull it off on Hispanic TV, I'd put a million dollars behind it."

We got the job and grew the Cable TV multicultural business from a division that lost forty million dollars a year, to selling one-point-five billion a year. And for the next five years, our little company, DMG Solutions, would generate more than twenty million dollars in income. We also helped create, launch, and manage several Hispanic TV networks.

We were financially independent and living a luxurious yet, thanks to Cindy, fiscally-responsible lifestyle in South Florida. Houses, condos, cars, and boats, all paid for in cash. No debt.

When our Cable TV client was audited for financial irregularities and left the company, they shut down the multicultural division and we were dismissed. So we closed our office doors, and I went to our beautiful waterfront penthouse in Key Largo to figure out the next phase of my life. That's when I read the prophetic book *The Alchemist* by Paulo Coelho.

For most of my adult life, I have tried to finish what I'd started, but one thing sat in the back of my mind: I have unfinished business in Gainesville.

Chapter 12

Back To College, Again

Cindy and I uprooted from the only place that ever felt like home, packed our belongings, and moved to what is still a strange, small, rural, college town.

We moved to Gainesville, Florida without a very clear plan, except I now wanted to be a college professor.

I would first have to finish my bachelor's degree, which would take at least eighteen months if I was to enroll full-time for four semesters. Then I'd need to get my master's degree, which would take another two years or so. And only then would I have the academic credentials to become a professor.

It was a good and romantic idea: re-inventing myself one last time. So I enrolled as an undergraduate student at the University of Florida in the fall of 2016, returning to finish my bachelor's degree.

The administrators at the College of Journalism seemed thrilled by the idea of me becoming a teacher, but they were concerned that I'd be bored as an undergraduate student at this stage of my life.

I personally thought it would be kind of cool, like the movie *The Intern*, where Robert De Niro gets to be the hip, old guy running around campus.

"How hard could this really be?" I thought. Sure, I'd be rusty at first, but I could push through it.

So I started what turned out to be my only semester with a full-time class load. After all, I was in a hurry to get my degrees and start teaching as soon as possible.

I took two advertising classes that I figured would be easy. I also enrolled in a journalism writing course, and a basic freshman-level statistics class. How hard could that be?

The first couple of weeks were daunting simply because of the newness and weirdness of it all. Parking spots were almost impossible to find, I didn't know where the bathrooms were, navigating around campus was dizzying at best, and I started thinking this was all designed to purposefully intimidate and thin the herd.

I attended every lecture, took copious notes, but I was seriously struggling with journalism and statistics by the third week.

I found a writing tutor to help with my journalism course. She was a bright student in her senior year who knew the subject well, and she agreed to work with me twice a week for a total of five hours.

I interviewed five possible tutors to help me with statistics, and narrowed the list to two before picking a young, doctoral student who agreed to work with me for six hours a week. After a couple of meetings with him, we upped it to fifteen hours a week, but I was still struggling.

Even though I attended the three-hour-long lectures and the two-hour labs every week, had a private tutor for three hours every morning, I was still having a hard time with Statistics.

When the third week rolled around, my tutor was by my side as I took the usual Thursday morning online quiz. I fumbled through the first couple of problems and started freaking out with my usual panic attack.

He stopped me and asked that I read the problem out loud, slowly. When I did, he said, "That is not what the problem says. Read it again."

So I read it again. And again he told me, "That is not what it says."

He noticed that I was inverting words, numbers, and symbols. I was doing it every single time I was asked to read the problem out loud.

"If you cannot read the questions or problems properly, you will never be able to answer them correctly, no matter how well you know the material."

I freaked out, froze, and started having a full-blown panic attack. He suggested I look at my notes and then try to answer the question, so I opened my workbook.

He looked at me with amazement and said, "What is this? I can't read it."

I couldn't either.

That was a defining moment for me.

I couldn't read my own notes, and could barely follow a class intended for eighteen-year-old kids who just graduated high school.

"What's going on with me?" I asked myself.

This single semester was one of the most defeating experiences of my life.

Chapter 13

The Struggle and Diagnosis

My three kids had all been diagnosed with -and treated for- ADHD. But as far as I was concerned, the whole ADHD thing sounded like "New Age" science; a bunch of millennial bunk to disguise laziness.

Could it be that I had an attention deficit disorder or a learning disability of some sort as well? What about all the inverted words, symbols, and numbers? And what was up with my notes?

At this point I had a lot more questions than answers.

I wandered into the College of Education office, where students were usually lined up to speak with their counselors and teachers. A nice, middle-aged woman greeted me in the reception area and asked me what was wrong.

As soon as I started to explain, the dean of the college walked right past us. I'd seen this man before; he and I were both on the board of a local non-profit.

He slowed his pace and said, "Jose, is that you? I didn't recognize you in those clothes."

Of course he didn't. I had only met him twice before, and both times I was in a suit-and-tie.

"What are you doing here?" He asked. "Can we help you with anything?"

I told the dean and the nice woman about my difficulties, and he asked me if I had ever been tested for learning disabilities. I told him that I hadn't, and that I didn't quite believe in the whole ADD thing.

He told me that lack of attention is pretty common, but inverting words and numbers sounded like dyslexia. The fact that I couldn't read my own notes sounded like something else altogether.

He told me about the university's Disabilities Resource Center (DRC), where I could get tested.

I set up a meeting at the DRC for evaluation, and carefully answered a questionnaire designed for initial screening. When I handed the completed questionnaire to the counselor, she placed the grading matrix over it and gave me a surprised look. "You just tested one hundred percent ADHD," she said. "I've never seen anything this certain."

"Let's discuss your options," she said. "In the state of Florida this classifies you as a person with a disability. You can take a smaller class load and still be considered a full-time student."

I didn't particularly like this idea, given that I was on a time-sensitive mission to finish school and start teaching as quickly as possible.

"You don't need to take your exams with the rest of the students, either. You can take your test here in our facilities, where you'll be given time-and-a-half instead of the usual allotted time for exams. Your teachers will provide you with the notes from their lectures, and the PowerPoint presentations that they use in the classroom. I will give you an accommodation letter that you must give to all of your professors."

With that, I felt some sense of relief. Perhaps I could navigate my classes moving forward. "But keep in mind that this is just a screener," she said. "The results were unequivocal so we can go ahead with an unofficial diagnosis right now, but you still need an official diagnosis."

She directed me to the university's Wellness Center for thorough testing. The Center was so overwhelmed by demand, however, that the earliest date they could test me was in a few months.

They told me I could reach out to private vendors if I wanted to get tested sooner, so I did exactly that.

I found a doctor who was conducting some of the leading-edge research in the field of neurological disorders, learning, and brain-wiring, and I made an appointment for testing in his private office.

The test lasted six hours, and consisted of reading, writing, pronunciation, spelling, and lip-reading. He told me I have severe ADHD, acute dyslexia, and some fine motor skills handicaps, especially connecting handwriting with vision.

"Bottom line," he said, "you should definitely drop out of school."

This was not what I had hoped to hear, but he explained that given my diagnosis, me completing my schoolwork would be like a 2-cylinder car in the middle of an Indy racetrack.

"It simply isn't doable," he said.

My heart sank.

I asked if there was any chance I could be fixed. And he said, "Of course! I can re-wire your brain, just like I have done for many others."

"How would that work?" I asked.

"First, you drop out of school for the next six months. I will write up the paperwork so you can go back when we're done. You will work with me and my staff Monday-Friday, eight hours a day, and we will re-wire your brain. You will be able to read any book you want after that. You'll be able to study law if you wanted to. Guaranteed."

"And what's all that going to cost me?" I asked.

"Well, that's kind of tricky," he said. "If you make a hundred-thousand dollar equity investment in my private firm, I will do all the work at no charge."

It sounded like someone was trying to fleece me out of a hundred grand, so that was the end of our relationship.

I found a different practitioner on the university's list of providers, a psychiatric practice that's been around the Gainesville area for several decades. The head of their learning disabilities testing was a middle-aged psychologist who took a particular interest in my life story and my aspirations to be a professor.

After the initial verbal evaluation ($200), I was asked to return for another appointment where I was going to be "officially" tested for my now-obvious learning disabilities. The test was in a small, quiet room, where they put a headset on me and asked me to click the computer mouse whenever I saw or heard certain letters, symbols, or sounds.

This test was very random. For the life of me I couldn't figure out if there was a pattern to any of it.

The test only took about thirty minutes, but my sight and sound sensitivity was pushed to the limit.

I remember telling the psychologist that I felt drained after the test. "That's very normal," she said to me. "Most people go home and rest afterwards."

The results would be back in a couple of days, and we would review them together at that time. It was starting to feel like another money pit.

"What do people without money do when they need to be diagnosed or treated?" I wondered. I realized how lucky I was to be able to afford this private testing, but many people just as desperate for answers cannot.

A few days later I went back to review my test results. I only scored twenty-eight percent on reading comprehension, which means I miss seventy-two percent of everything I read.

But there was some good news: I scored a hundred-and-eighty percent on listening comprehension, which means I learn better through listening, not reading.

This is why I was able to play the guitar by ear but couldn't read sheet music to save my life. Things finally started making sense.

I felt extremely vulnerable. I was broken.

I talked to the therapist about my results, the dyslexia, and the motor skills issues, and she confirmed that these were pretty common accompaniments to ADHD.

"They tend to travel in packs," she said.

Nearly twenty percent of the population has some form of learning disability. There must be a treatment for it, right?

"The treatment is experimental and hit-or-miss until the exact dosage of the right medication is figured out," she explained. "It greatly varies by each individual. Most of the treatments are amphetamine, salt-based medications."

So not only was I broken, but the treatment involved experimental drugs.

Getting addicted to amphetamines with my drug history at almost age sixty did not seem like a step towards neurological health.

I was angry, wondering if I should even bother. But I had weathered worse storms in the past, and I could weather this one as well.

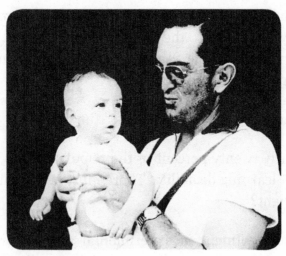

With my dad, before breaking

Chapter 14

Bad or Broken?

Once I was "officially" diagnosed with ADHD, dyslexia, and a fine motor skill disability, I returned to the Disabilities Resource Center on campus, and my personal record was updated.

This ensured that I would receive the state-mandated accommodations offered to special students like myself.

Relieved, I walked into my counselor's office and said, "Jane, I no longer think of myself as a bad person; I'm just broken!"

She looked puzzled and asked, "Why did you ever think you were bad in the first place?"

I wasn't going to tell her the particular details of a lifetime trying to ignore comments like, "You are not only the devil's son, you are the devil himself."

Almost sixty years of hearing "You are a bad person" can take its toll. If I had learned anything from my profession in advertising, it was the undeniable fact that repetition sells. The industry calls it "frequency of messaging." You repeat something enough times and people will start believing it.

My mother's mother had physically and emotionally abused her own daughter, sent her to a religious boarding school when she was young, until one day my mother finally broke and became a junkie.

And when it came time to raise me, my mother didn't see me as a defenseless child, she saw a perfect target for her anger and guilt. She was broken, repeating the same programmed behavior patterns.

My father's family appeared okay on the surface, but they were also dysfunctional. My father must have been broken himself, but I wasn't old enough to understand how these issues presented themselves in our family.

I know my father's father had neglected his children and his wife, and probably had great expectations from his son. My grandparents divorced while my father was still in college, and I know he was greatly affected by this; broken.

When I met Cindy, I straightened out my act and got my life together. Through a lot of hard work, dedication, and outside support, I somehow made it out okay.

What's I've discovered about my life has finally sparked some compassion for myself from myself.

So I began to say, "I am not a bad person, I am broken." Perhaps like everybody else.

This is not an easy thing to share, but letting my guard down, and showing myself to the world as I truly am: vulnerable and broken, seems like a form of exoneration. It feels like a declaration of innocence.

I am not bad, and some of the incredibly bad stuff that has happened in my life is because we are all a little broken. That is the lesson I have come to accept: we are all broken, just in different ways.

I think declaring this about myself is a form of surrender. Not in the sense of weakness, but in humility about my own condition. There is no point in making an enemy of myself.

The war is over!

With my mother, 1973

Chapter 15

Troubled Ties: Trauma and Learning Disabilities

The Centers for Disease Control and Prevention, together with the Kaiser Permanente Medical Care Program, the University of Arizona, and Emory University in Georgia, conducted a major health study exploring the relationship between childhood traumatic experiences and physical/emotional/mental ailments. What they found was a direct correlation and unequivocal evidence linking the two: the more childhood trauma one experiences, the higher the probability of a person developing acute health issues later in life. It was not just correlation but causation.

The Adverse Childhood Experiences Study (ACE) demonstrated an association of adverse childhood experiences (ACEs) with health and social problems. Dr. Robert Block, the former President of the American Academy of Pediatrics, considers childhood trauma to be the most overlooked public health threat that is currently facing our nation.

How would you know if you have trauma-induced learning disabilities? The ACE screening is a simple, ten-question test, and the result is the number you score out of ten.

Most Americans have one or two ACEs, and they get to lead pretty normal lives. But the moment your ACE score starts climbing into the fours and fives, your chances of suicide, for example, are already twelve times higher.

Twelve times higher!

And if you score a six or a seven, you are almost definitely going to end up in jail or dead. It's pretty straightforward stuff; not very fancy, and not very pretty, either.

I serve on the board of directors for an incredible community-based not-for-profit organization that takes care of foster children and adoptions in the Northern Central Florida region. It's an organization called Partnership for Strong Families (PSF), a real and important solution to heart-wrenching situations.

When the sheriff's office yanks children away from their home in the middle of the night because of reported child abuse or neglect, they place the kids in our care, and it's our job to manage those kids' lives until they are eighteen.

It is far from a foolproof process, but it plays an incredibly important role in society. To give some context, PSF serves thousands of children from thirteen counties in Northern Central Florida.

Pause for a moment and think about that: there are thousands of displaced kids in a small, rural, lightly populated part of Florida. Can you imagine the scale of the problem on a national level? The affected population is in the millions!

A few months ago, during a day-long board of directors' retreat, our CEO handed us the ACE test, together with the accompanying study as a reference, just so we'd all be aware of how we test our population of children and parents to see what kind of hand they'd been dealt. The more traumatized the subject, the more health problems they are going to face.

Our CEO is an extremely knowledgeable man in this field. He has overseen the Department of Children's Welfare in the State of Florida for many years, been running PSF for a decade, and as a judge, he has seen these cases in Tallahassee. All in all, he has been involved in the field of traumatized children for over thirty years.

I took the ACE test out of curiosity, and scored a nine out of the ten possible Adverse Childhood Experiences in my life.

"You're not supposed to be alive," he said to me. "Do you realize that?"

Childhood trauma changes our brain architecture forever. And stress keeps the "fear center" of the brain on high alert while other parts of the brain are underdeveloped, which later causes problems with focus and learning.

I always thought these things were passed to children in their genetic code, not caused by trauma. So when I first learned about this, I felt angry, depressed, and confused. I was a product of toxic, childhood trauma, which lead to my learning disabilities and drug addiction.

When my father died, I was in third grade. I had been an honor student and well-behaved until that point. By the fourth, fifth, and sixth grade, however, the first signs of trauma-induced learning disabilities began to present themselves. The teachers thought my father's death was perhaps too much for me to handle, but my ability to learn was actually changing. I could no longer keep up with the other kids.

The trauma, disabilities, and my grades, all got progressively worse when I left for boarding school and then high school. I initially blamed the weed, but now I know better.

In today's world I would be prescribed Adderall or some other amphetamine to help me focus. Without even realizing it, I was self-medicating with marijuana to get me through tests and help me complete homework assignments without getting sidetracked.

When I was a business owner and had employees, they all knew that I only had the attention span of a two-year-old. "You need to talk to Joe in short phrases," they would say. "Get to the point quickly; he has zero patience." That was clearly my unmitigated Attention Deficit Hyperactive Disorder, I just didn't know it by name.

"Joe has the handwriting of a doctor," was the ongoing joke amongst my colleagues. "Don't let Joe near the white board around clients, no one can read his writing." That was my motor-skills disabilities in all their glory, but who knew?

I have somehow managed to lead an extraordinary life, and pulled off an almost impossible task against the odds. Disabilities and all.

A friend recently asked me if I believe in God.

"The fact that I am still alive, walking, and talking, is a miracle in and of itself," I told her. "I'd love for you to read my life story some day, and I bet you'd also believe in a higher power if you don't already."

The only constant throughout my life was the "hand of God." He appeared in my father, my grandfather, my uncle, my landlord, and so many others, most of whom were broken themselves, but they managed to save my life in one way or another.

I feel a moral obligation to tell my story. Unvarnished, raw, and vulnerable.

There are millions of us broken-but-not-bad folks out there, not knowing what's wrong with us. I want to impart some hope that everything is going to be alright.

In fact, everything **is** alright. Disabilities and all.

Chapter 16

What We Know, and How We Can Help

Learning disabilities are an inconvenient truth for many of us.

Parents struggle with any child who learns at a different pace or behaves differently from their siblings, neighbors, and classmates. They often think their child might be somehow broken, and the guilt associated with having a broken child is often far greater than a parents' will to have their child tested, diagnosed, and treated.

One of the myths about learning disabilities is that they are strictly genetically transmitted, and no parent wants to take the blame for passing bad or broken genes to their children.

Compounding fears of the unknown are also a big factor. "What would it take to fix my child? How much will it cost?"

Other parents either in complete denial about the symptoms, or they worry that labeling their child with a disability would cause even more harm.

But it's a tragedy of epic proportions that we can't afford to ignore. According to the National Institute of Health, fifteen to twenty percent of Americans are affected with a wide range of learning disabilities and attention disorders.

Some educators of K-12 are still in denial about the reality of learning disabilities, and they continue to call out children who cannot keep up with the rest of the class, or complete their assigned work or curriculum. This can stress the child even more, and make the problem worse.

As far as higher education institutions are concerned (from community colleges to state-run universities), learning disabilities are simply bad for business. Eighty percent of higher education providers in the U.S. are public/state-funded, tax supported institutions. A percentage of tax revenue collected is earmarked for public education, so colleges are only given tuition reimbursement if they meet the scoring numbers imposed by the state. And students with learning disabilities throw off their numbers.

Our society wants to turn a blind eye, and doesn't want to hear that our children are being traumatized, yet sixty percent of adults report that they, themselves, were abused in their childhood. Twenty-six percent of children in the United States witness or experience a traumatic event before they turn four; and forty percent of children in America report some form of physical assault in the past year.

Trauma-Induced Learning Disabilities are the double espresso of mental health and learning disabilities in our society.

Only by addressing the problem as a collective, social epidemic can we hope to affect any real change.

What can we do?

First, we need to be honest with ourselves and with our children, and accept that the problem exists.

Second, we need to be present. We need to look for the telltale signs of brokenness, misbehavior, irregular school performance, and trouble with certain subjects. We need to listen to our children.

Third, we must change the labels we use when dealing with a child who learns differently. We are all too quick to call them "bad" or "lazy," when in reality, that child is giving her/his best. They may not be properly wired to learn like other kids. We need to quit calling them "bad." They are simply broken, and they can be treated to excel in our society in many ways.

Fourth, we need to be brave and get our children tested. We must not be afraid of the stigma that comes with learning disabilities and childhood traumatic experiences. Realize that the earlier you diagnose a learning disability or childhood trauma, the sooner you can start treating it.

Last of all, we need to have compassion for our broken brothers and sisters, whether they are innocent children or abusive adults. They are suffering.

We must also have compassion for ourselves when we're scared to look this monster in the eye.

Our children may have some disabilities, but they often develop exceptional skills to compensate for those disabilities.

If we look at the problems as opportunities, we'd start seeing their disabilities as super-abilities.

Chapter 17

Coping Through Prayer and Meditation

There are things I do to make myself feel more grounded, namely a prayer practice each morning, and meditation every afternoon.

As often as possible, I combine my morning prayer practice with an exercise routine, which gives me a double shot of dopamine ("feel-good" endorphins).

I use one of seven different prayers that I've collected throughout my life, ranging from Christian to Buddhist, or I simply reflect on my life's journey as a form of loving kindness and compassion. Looking at pictures from various stages of my life, I honor the courage it took to survive each one.

No day is complete without my morning prayer. Regardless of where I am or what is going on, I make time to reflect and contemplate. Being broken requires a lot of healing.

In the afternoons I sit in a quiet place or listen to soothing music, and I practice letting go of my thoughts and anxieties.

A wonderful mindfulness and meditation teacher in Miami named Alice has taught me many life lessons, and has been a guiding light and mentor to me for several years.

The most important lesson she taught me was that we need to make peace within ourselves before we can promote it without. I now send compassionate thoughts and prayers to myself, knowing that we are all a little broken. We are all looking for a little peace within ourselves.

"God is not 'out there,' God is right inside each and every one of us," reads one of my Franciscan daily reflections.

So I focus on staying right here and right now. There is nowhere else I need to be, there is nowhere else I need to go, and there is nothing else I need to do.

Following are my daily meditation prayers and mantras. These are phrases that I silently go through in sequence with my eyes closed, trying to clear my head of all thoughts outside these words.

May I feel compassion for myself now.

May I be relieved from my pain and suffering now.

May my worries and anxieties subside now.

May I be okay when I feel like I don't fit-in.

May I be okay when I feel scared or detached.

May I know and feel deep in my heart and in my
soul that this very moment, this very instant,
is the only place, the perfect place, for me to fit
into right now.

May I have compassion for myself now.

May I be safe now.

May I be free from any internal or external harm.

May I be happy now.

May I feel peace and calm.

May I be healthy in my body and physical space.

May I be healthy in my mind and in my thoughts.

May I be healthy in my spirit and in my soul.

May I live with ease now.

May my day-to-day living be without struggle.

May I feel love and be loving at all times.

May I learn to love myself more.

I thank you, Lord, for everything you give to me.

I love you so much, Lord!

I close my days with a short gratitude practice. At age forty-two, when I'd lost everything, a Brazilian co-worker offered me the same guidance that he had learned from his father, a humble and highly spiritual man in his own personal and traditional ways:

"Don't go to sleep like a man and wake up a horse."

Translation: go to sleep like a man, and wake up like a man; a grateful man! Replay the day in your mind to find things and moments, big or small, that you are grateful for. Fall asleep counting your blessings, not sheep.

To this day, that is one of the simplest, yet most useful practices I have. Start with small things like gratitude for the taste of coffee in the morning, or clean drinking water. Once you get into the groove, you will find many things to be grateful for. The most powerful forces in the universe are love and gratitude.

Some eastern religions and philosophies like Buddhism call it "finding joy" in everything, even in bad and broken things.

In the words of my Franciscan mentor: "God stands in solidarity with all the pain and suffering in the universe, allowing us to be participants in our own healing."

Chapter 18

Joe's Five Lessons

The following five reminders continue to guide me, and they can serve as an instruction manual of sorts for fixing things whenever they break.

1. **Forgive generously**.

   Forgive everyone who hurt you in the past, those who are currently hurting you, and everyone who will hurt you in the future.

   Realize that you did not provoke the pain, betrayal, or any of the things you suffer from; it's not your fault.

   Forgive yourself for all the people you've hurt in the past, the ones you are hurting in the present, and everyone you will unintentionally but inevitably hurt in the future.

2. **Be present**.

Find all the things you can be grateful for in this very moment. This is the only moment that really exists. This very breath cycle is all we've got.

The past is just a dream; we must practice letting things go when they only cause more misery.

The future is a mirage, an illusion that can rob us of our happiness in the present moment by worrying about something that doesn't even exist.

3. **Thank your higher power**.

"Seek and you shall find; ask and you shall receive."

Ask your higher power to hold your hand, and you will be held. Thank your higher power for keeping your head above water.

4. **It's okay to let go**.

Let go of all your past trauma, disappointments, and betrayals; none of it serves a higher purpose in your life.

Loosen your tight grip of the present moment because it will soon be gone. Stay fluid.

And let go of future worries as well. The secret to a happy life is enjoying the passage of time. So make the most of each day as it goes by without trying to cling to it.

5. **Surrender**.

Take your life, all the events in it, all the joy and all the pain, and offer it up to God.

Surrender yourself to a higher power, to the wisdom of the infinite. Let it guide your life; it will anyway. You are safe in its care.

Florida Keys, 2015

Chapter 19

Give Peace a Chance

Uprooting myself from the American Dream-like life in South Florida, after more than three decades of building it, has repeatedly made me ask myself: Why?

For example: Why Gainesville?

I first came here on sabbatical to write this book. It has offered me context for the life I've had, and given me a better understanding of myself, how my "brokenness" came about, and why I couldn't finish college.

Although I thought I was moving here to eventually share my career knowledge of marketing and advertising with students at the university, perhaps what I was always meant to share was my story. That is my real body of work, after all; advertising and marketing are just my profession.

If what I share can comfort or even slightly ease the pain of a single broken person, then it was all worth the journey.

Perhaps I had to come here to declare peace with myself and to exonerate myself of my past actions. I have found resolution, absolution, redemption, and liberation from my own convoluted history.

Gainesville is where I let go of my beloved guitar many years ago, and where I gave up on my creative energy. This book is my manifesto of hope. As broken as my story is, I hope it helps others with similar challenges; others who are suffering, who need help.

In writing this book, I now know that I was worthy of love despite it all. That is my biggest wish for anyone else who is broken out there, struggling to understand.

I wish you love, acceptance, and God's peace on your journey.

— Joe

Pause and Remember:

No one is coming to
rescue you from yourself,
your inner demons,
your lack of confidence,
your dissatisfaction with your self or life.
Only self-love and
good decisions will rescue you.

— Jenni Young

CPSIA information can be obtained
at www.ICGtesting.com
Printed in the USA
BVOW09s0101211117
500905BV00004B/595/P